# A History of Western Philosophy in a Nutshell

## plus commentary

# A History of Western Philosophy in a Nutshell

## plus commentary

### Donald Mangum

Half Inch Press

# Contents

*For Cynthia, Jessi, and John*

# Preface

The following is a sketch, a connect-the-dots narrative, the dots being the big names and the big ideas that drove the history of (mainly continental) Western philosophy from its beginning in ancient Greece to the peak of the existentialist movement during the first half of the twentieth century. For the most part, the level of depth is intended for anyone wishing to acquire at least a passing familiarity with the philosophers and concepts commonly referenced in a wide range of discourse. As a narrative, it is as readable as I could make it. Its brevity, of course, comes partly at the cost of selective omissions and radical condensations, some of which would likely horrify certain scholars. For example, a serious Aristotelian would probably shudder at the limited treatment of Aristotle. There is no mention at all of classical pragmatism. And some philosophers undoubtedly get a more detailed treatment than necessary for a passing familiarity. (In these instances, the content seemed to warrant greater elaboration.)

In addition, many of the strictly historical sections are separated by commentary. These come without apology. I hope they provide some perspective.

"The unexamined life is not worth living."

Socrates


"For in much wisdom is much vexation, and he who
increases knowledge increases sorrow."
— *Ecclesiastes*


"A thinker is now that being in whom the impulse for
truth and those life-preserving errors now clash for
their first fight, after the impulse for truth has proved
to be also a life-preserving power. . . .To what extent
can truth endure incorporation? That is the question;
that is the experiment."
Friedrich Nietzsche, *The Gay Science*

# Introduction: What Is Philosophy?

Often when people make rude remarks about my drinking, I tell them I have a degree in philosophy. This usually silences them, but when not, I add that at least I'm not a sports fan, to which an acquaintance (Bobby, a sports fan) once replied, and with some temerity, what exactly is philosophy, anyway?

It's a fair question, with no short answer. It's not like *What is biology?* or *What is math?* In biology, you study physical life. In math, numbers. But what do you study in philosophy? Philosophy is unique among fields of study in that you can't define it by its subject matter. Furthermore, you can be philosophical about practically anything, including physical life and numbers.

So to answer (Bobby), let me begin with an equally fair question: what is science? Given the recent prominence of the term in the arena of public debate, what are people talking about when they refer to "the science" behind, say, cries about global warming or the CDC's latest recommendations? I dare say that of the general horde of the outspoken, very few mean anything more specific than whatever it is that scientists do or, more likely, say. But to the point of the first question, it wasn't until the late 19th century that the term *science* came to replace *natural philosophy* to refer to the investigation of natural phenomena. The need for a name change was largely precipitated by developments in methodology. The study of nature, it was recognized, seemed to yield a dependable sort of results when conducted with a methodological rigor involving controlled and repeatable experimentation, among other empirical means. Think of this splintering off of science as key to what the term *philosophy* refers to. The various branches of philosophy (ethics, metaphysics, epistemology, etc.) tend to focus on problems which lie beyond the reach of empirical experimentation. *How does the world work?* is a question for science. Observe, gather data, form a hypothesis, perform experiments, repeat. *Why does the world exist? Why is there something rather than nothing? What is the meaning of existence, especially my own?* Pretty much all you can do with these questions is to think. Now you're philosophizing.

# The Beginning of Philosophy



Historians of Western philosophy see something of a beginning in a conjecture by *Thales* that *everything is water.* (Picture this: Mid-sixth century B. C., a man is standing on the edge of a grassy marsh, wiggling his toes in the mud. In the distance is water. Behind him is land. At his feet, some combination of the two emits a sulfurous gas, pungent, eggy. He thinks how here the water seems to become land, or else land becomes water. Or both. Water, he thinks. Mud. Earth. Flora, fauna, stones, mountains. Rain. Now imagine Richard Strauss's *Thus Spoke Zarathustra* beginning its slow crescendo toward the dawn of man as, in a revelation of a profundity not experienced before or perhaps since, he thinks, *everything is really water.*) The event reflects the beginning of the end of a way of looking at the world, a way gradually to be replaced by philosophy and later by its offshoot science. Prior to that time, myths were humankind's means for explaining the world and negotiating our relationship with it. Nature was seen as a mere façade for the gods, anthropomorphic entities with whom our relationships were interpersonal affairs, totally unlike the objectification of the world that comes automatically with our modern scientistic point of view. Zeus, Poseidon, Apollo, and their like were the agents behind doom or fortune – the great roiling caldron of nature and of our lives in it. (Remember when you were a child, and you'd look at a rock and try to imagine its total lack of awareness, and you couldn't, and you thought surely somehow that rock is thinking *I am rock*? That's called *animism,* often a part of primitive collective consciousness as well as a child's.) Hence, the beginning of philosophy marks the initial waning of humankind's interpersonal relationship with the world. Primarily, what's significant about water is not its selection from among many substances, but rather the fact that *water is not a god and doesn't care about you.*

In addition, the statement that everything is *really* water is the first known instance of an intuitive conviction that *all things are one,* a conviction that survives to this day. The idea that all the structures of matter as well as forms of energy can be further and further reduced, issuing ultimately from a singularity coincident with the "big bang," is but the latest in two and a half millennia of philosophical attempts to explain the *many* in terms of the *one*. What was Einstein's commitment to finding a unified field theory if not a philosophical intuition?

Two more directions of thought come with Thales' philosophical bombshell. Since obviously many things appear to be other than water, to say that everything is *really* water implies a radical and fundamental difference between *appearance* and *reality*. Water is *real*. All the dynamic permutations of the world of appearance are just that, appearance. *Mere* appearance. (In case this seems too far removed from common sense to take seriously, remember that many physicists since Einstein have insisted that time as we experience it is an illusion.)

As well there is a presumed *permanence* to the state of reality which underlies the world. For future reference, this underlying *permanence* is often referred to as *being* as opposed to the *flux*, or *becoming*, of the world of experience.

Philosophy, then, has its genesis in a gradual waning of one way of looking at the world – *mythical* – in favor of another, one that involves a greater reliance on human powers of observation and reasoning. Also, tied to this break there is a three-fold opposition (to be joined later by a fourth): (1) *unity versus multiplicity*, (2) *reality versus appearance*, and (3) *stasis (being) versus flux (becoming)*.

## Commentary: The Loss

Philosophy and science come at a cost. With mythic consciousness, the relationship with the world is personal. Nature is informed, not by abstract principles, but by the gods. The world is itself sacred, a haunt for beings divine but still like us. It is the medium between the mortal and the immortal, a place where simply to be is to have meaning. But to say that everything is water is to reduce the world, and yourself as well, to a lifeless substance. As Unamuno says, "In order to understand anything, it is necessary to kill it, to lay it out rigid in the mind." Thus, to know the world is to inject it with a mental venom. To dissect it, we first have to kill it, and in the process, we create a kind of death in life. To quote Wordsworth (though he was talking more about commerce than about science/philosophy):

> . . . Great God! I'd rather be
> A Pagan suckled in a creed outworn;
> So might I, standing on this pleasant lea,
> Have glimpses that would make me less
> forlorn;
> Have sight of Proteus rising from the sea;
> Or hear old Triton blow his wreathèd horn.

A looming question is, Do we kill the world out of a desire to know it, or do we know the world out of a desire to kill it? Readers of Flannery O'Connor might think immediately of Hulga, a physically grotesque character with a PhD in philosophy, who is obsessed with the absurdity of life. But in a kind of self-deluding denial, she intellectualizes that absurdity and thus from the lofty remove of philosophy manages to berate life from the point of view of her own transcendent orbit. She attempts to kill the world out of pure resentment.

Or consider the hot young grad student in literature who prefers talking about bad art than good, delighting in their own learned dissection and reduction of a work into its sources, form, tradition, what not, though they personally have never written or even loved a single work of beauty. Deconstructionism comes particularly to mind as a veiled product of resentment with its insistence that all of art – all of life – is in principle deconstructable, reducible to the basest and most lifeless elements.

Of course, the point isn't to dismiss philosophy/science (or arts criticism) because of its misuse by an insidious and loose affiliation of killjoys. Still, it bears keeping in mind that often where analysis ends, mystery begins.

# Presocratics



To the three-fold opposition that comes with the birth of philosophy, add a fourth with Anaximander and with the uneven progress of philosophy through the time of the Presocratics: *reason* (or *understanding*) *versus experience* (or *sense perception*). Anaximander held that the one real being underlying the multiform flux of appearance was what he called the *apeiron,* or *boundless* substance. Significantly, the *apeiron* cannot be experienced through the senses; rather, it can be known only through the pure exercise of *reason.*

The problem with water as the ultimate basis of reality, Anaximander reasoned, is that it is an identifiable substance among other identifiable substances. It is limited by its specific characteristics (its *essence,* as we might say now) which make it what it is rather than something else. The fundamental substance underlying all others, he thought, must not be limited by any specific identity -- must itself have no particular qualities -- but serve only as a substrate for the sensible things of the everyday world.

Anaximander's thinking is considered the first true *metaphysics*. Whereas Thales presumably drew on his sense experience of, for example, the relative wetness of the various forms of stuff, Anaximander's *apeiron* is neither suggested nor testable by experience.

Then in a step backwards from pure metaphysics, Anaximenes again resorts to physical observation of nature to determine that *air* must be the ultimate stuff, adding that the constant coming and going of all the different forms (things) of appearance may be explained according to the processes of condensation and rarefaction (thus we have to put a coaster between the coke can and the coffee table because the air will condense into water and run down the can to mess up the table). And dirt and rocks are even denser than water, and so on. Here Anaximenes at least sees the need to explain *how* the most fundamental substance becomes this that or the other. He identifies a specific process to account for change. And perhaps even more importantly, Anaximenes points out that even the gods are subject to the processes of condensation and rarefaction of air. Even the gods are air. In so saying, Anaximenes severs one more line tying humans to myth in their view of themselves and the world. The gods are still around, but they are now explicitly relegated to a status closer to those of us and the world. Gods are no longer the ultimate reasons that things are as they are. As mere mortals, we can know by our own devices what makes the world the world, gods and all.

Thales, Anaximander, and Anaximenes were all monists; that is, they all believed that there is one fundamental something underlying all the multiple forms of the world of experience. Now, before we get to Parmenides, the most profound and venerated of the monists, the giant of the Pre-socratics, at least a cursory glance at the camp of *pluralists* is in order (not chronological) as well as some mention of the cultish group of *Pythagoreans* and the somewhat lone-wolf figure of *Heraclitus*.

As the name implies, *pluralism* is the belief in a plurality of elemental types. For example, *Anaxagoras* reasoned that everything is made out of *seeds* and that there is a kind of seed for every type of thing. Good things are good by virtue of the purity of their make-up. For example, good cats have a higher percentage of cat seeds than do bad cats, which may have a portion of dog seeds, or perhaps monkey. Empedocles held that all things consist of different combinations of *earth, air, fire,* and *water,* which are determined in their arrangements by *love* and *strife.* He suspected that plants have sex (although probably not very good), and he died by jumping into Mount Aetna, an active volcano. You may also consider the *atomists* as pluralists (or not). For example, *Leucippus* and *Democritus* believed that tiny *indivisible* (*atom* is Greek for *indivisible*) *particles*, presumably of the same stuff (hence the problem with applying the term *pluralism*), compose all things. What is most philosophically significant about the atomists, however, is not how modern sounding the idea of an atom might seem, but rather what was thought to separate the individual atoms: nothingness. And that was, and still is, a problematic concept, as we will see with Parmenides.

*Heraclitus*, often quoted but seldom agreed upon, was a misfit among the Presocratics. His writings survive only in fragments which tend to be as enigmatic as they are insightful. One point of agreement, however, is that he is the first *process* philosopher, which would make him more at home in the 20th century A.D. than in the 6th century B.C. Of the surviving fragments, the two by which he is most identified are as follows: (1) "This world-order (kosmos), the same for all, no god nor man did create, but it ever was and is and will be: ever-living fire, kindling in measures and being quenched in measures." (2) "No man ever steps in the same river twice, for it is not the same river and he is not the same man." It is hard to believe that Heraclitus meant literally that the world is a *fire*, although that is the word that comes inevitably and first to mind when people think of Heraclitus. But the point is that, unlike water, *apeiron,* and air, *fire is a process and not a substance.* Another fragment reads, "All things are in flux," and while there is a *unifying principle,* or *logos,* it is *process* or *flux* or *change* that is fundamental to the world, and this idea places Heraclitus in a Presocratic eddy of thought for his time, as the main current was towards permanence in the permanence/flux opposition.

The *Pythagoreans,* as the name implies, comprised a group of followers of Pythagoras (of the well-known "theorem," though the belief that Pythagoras first discovered it is demonstrably false). They tended to be cultish, secretive, and ritualistic in their practices and beliefs. They blended religion and philosophy in a way one might wish they hadn't, but their worship of *numbers* seems now to have anticipated Plato's metaphysics of the higher reality of incorporeal entities. Their discoveries in the mathematics of harmony were inflated to the status of a cosmology, *"the music of the spheres"* as it is known, a belief that the cosmos literally moved in musically harmonic order. But what stands out most is their view of *fundamental reality as incorporeal. Mathematical entities have specific, nonarbitrary characteristics and are therefore as real as you or I.* Or more so.

Which brings us to *Parmenides,* in whose poem (dactylic hexameter, surviving only in fragments) the four oppositions of Presocratic philosophy are resolved in the concept of reality as *one unchanging being* known only by *reason* and inaccessible by sensory experience. Modern readers, translators, and historians of philosophy have made noble attempts to extract from Parmenides's poem at least a respectable argument that change is not real. Here is yet another:

> Thought itself is always *of something*.
> Thus *nothingness* is literally *unthink-*
> *able* (for *nothing* is not *something*).
> (And here comes the crucial step.)
> Since *nothing(ness) is unthinkable,*
> any belief that requires belief in
> *nothing(ness)* is therefore false.

From here he goes on to argue that *change (becoming) is mere appearance and not real,* since changing would require that a thing's constituent properties would become nothing as the new properties replaced them. And as for the many (plurality), the many would have to be parts of Being itself, but for there to be parts of Being, there would have to be nothing(ness) separating them. Since nothing(ness) is unthinkable, so is plurality. If experience tells you that reality is made up of many things changing, then you must reject your experience as a source of truth because *what is real is one eternal changeless being accessible only by the understanding and not by experience.* Of course for any of this reasoning to work, it must be assumed that *understanding and reality are isomorphic* (of the same form).

In the same vein, Zeno, a student of Parmenides, maintained that motion is impossible by pointing out certain absurdities in the implications. For example, to travel any distance, something must go halfway first. But to go even that distance, it must likewise go halfway first, and on and on for an infinite number of halfway points. Of course, infinity is limitless, so to go any distance is to go beyond the limit of the limitless, which goes against the laws of thought and hence is not within the realm of possibility.

## Commentary: Rationality as an Act of Faith

Parmenides's argument represents the culmination of a growing audaciousness among the Presocratics. What begins with Thales as the bud of a revolution against the gods at last finds its most profound manifestation in the ultimate renunciation of common sense and of the sum of experience as sources of true knowledge. Which are you going to believe, Parmenides asks, me (as the voice of reason) or your lying eyes? Choose one: one eternal, unchanging, featureless Being that reason insists must obtain as the true reality, or the great multifaceted whirl of experience, with all its joy and tragedy, its life and death, and love and heartache and the slings and the arrows of fortune and time's endless fire, the whole roiling world that you have always accepted as what there was. Then explain your choice.

But first consider another choice, made centuries later. The existence of kings and slaves, of geniuses and morons, of Goliaths and Tiny Tims, is pretty convincing evidence that we are not all created equal. So what on Earth were the signers of the Declaration of Independence thinking when they endorsed a document reading: "We hold these truths to be self-evident, that all men are created equal"? *Self-evident?* Both history and experience tell us that life is ranked, among the beasts by the food chain, and in humanity, not only by the structure of society itself, but by natural differences in both physical and mental abilities. The clear evidence is that we are created on a scale of ability and worth.

*Equal? Self-evident?*

I submit that for the signers of the Declaration, *self-evident meant that in the absence of any outside evidence, and in fact, in the face of all evidence to the contrary, we will commit ourselves to this proposition and to a new nation founded on this proposition, and at the risk of our very existence.* In other words, *we hold these truths to be articles of faith.*

# Socrates



Sorting out Socrates the man from Socrates the character in Plato's dialogues might be a problem for historians of philosophy, but philosophically, what difference does it make? In fact, the Socratic spirit would suggest that the question is silly. And yet the actual historical figure deserves some gratitude for much of what is undoubtedly his legacy.

First, the precept that *the unexamined life is not worth living* is by its nobility alone enough to make up for what it lacks in either intuitive or popular appeal. (After all there's no guarantee that the examined life *is* worth living.) In fact, the link between wisdom and vexation is so pervasive in literature as to hardly require pointing out. For now, then, let us add Socrates's primary dictum to the same bucket with Parminedes's reason and the U. S. founding fathers' notion of human equality: let us call it an article of faith.

Second, *Socratic wisdom* is the awareness of one's own ignorance. A recent related point is made with the Dunning-Kruger effect, in which a person's estimation of their own competence/expertise tends to be inversely proportional to their actual, or to quote the Bard, "The fool doth think he is wise."

Socrates made it his business to expose the purported intelligentsia of his day as the fools they truly were, and of course was sentenced to death for his troubles.

Third, the *Socratic method* is a tactic of teaching by asking the right questions, allowing the student to dis(un)cover the knowledge for themselves. In mathematics especially, instruction is in effect a matter of guiding a person through their "memory" of eternal truths.

### Commentary: Socrates and Jesus

Socrates is also well known for his willing death by hemlock as the sentence for the trumped-up charges by the state (corruption of the youth, atheism, whatever). He is venerated even today as much for the way he died as for the way he lived. What he is not known for is what he wrote, which if anything at all, might as well be nothing. Why?

Jesus of Nazareth, God in the flesh (as held by the largest religion on Earth), was another historical figure known as much for his death as for his life, who curiously never wrote a word that survived him. Why?

Is it because both Jesus and Socrates knew that love has to work without a net, the net being the law and/or scripture for the religious and the written text for the philosopher? Of course Christian denominations and factions will always wrangle over the letter of the Word, while analytic philosophers continue to dissect and disaggregate, all probably to the betterment of their respective understandings. Certainly exegesis serves up to a certain point, but where the letter falls short, the spirit may continue to shine through the likes of love, faith, relentless examinations through deliberation and dialectic, or – who knows? – art.

Notably, philosophy is one of only two academic disciplines with the word *phil* in its name. (*Philosophy* means "love of wisdom" in Greek, the other discipline being *philology*, which means "love of words.") Also notable is that love, ineffability, and transcendence tend to bear various associations in the contexts of philosophy, religion, and art. In a sense, the higher the realm one attains, the more rarified becomes the language. In the end, there is no Love by the Book, a lesson that both Jesus and Socrates may have left by their lives.

# Plato and Aristotle

In the center of Raphael's painting titled *The School of Athens*, Plato and Aristotle famously walk side by side, Plato pointing upwards while Aristotle gestures, palm downwards, in metaphorical references to the realms of the real. Of metaphysics, Plato and Aristotle are the cat and dog respectively. Plato is abstracted and spiritual, maintaining a sort of feline transcendence, often playful but only on his own terms (operating with the indirection of the playwright, the artist, crouching behind characters, advancing in fits and starts), batting an idea about often long after it has died, subtle, wry, and always the stylist. He is at home with mystery and at peace with silence. Aristotle, on the other hand, seeks truth and reality in immanence, bounding like a lab retriever into the swamp water of experience. For him there is no irony, no winks at the reader, no boredom with moderation or in the endless plodding progress of dry logic and common sense. He is a codifier of thought and an auditor of life, an accountant at heart. Never doubting the isomorphism of language, thought, and reality, he slogs his way through nearly two hundred treatises.

# Plato

*hierarchy of being*
*Platonic forms*
*analogies of the divided line, the cave, and the sun*

In Plato's metaphysics and epistemology, we find resolutions to the four-fold Presocratic oppositions (one/many, permanence/flux, reality/appearance, and understanding/experience) in a *hierarchy* of reality and knowledge; that is, reality and knowledge themselves have planes, or tiers, of superiority, ranging from the lowest (multiplicious, changing, and experienced by the senses) to the highest (unified, permanent or eternal, and apprehended by the understanding). Moreover, each of these planes owes its very manifestation to the plane above it as something like an emanation (or reflection?) from higher to lower. The most general division in these tiers of reality is between the *formal* and the *material* or *physical*. The formal realm is abstract, conceptual, and ideal. It is associated with reason or the understanding. It is also the means by which things in the material or physical world are recognized. The *material (physical)* realm is made up of individual, concrete objects of sensory experience or specific events. Thus, a *Platonic form* is the form, idea, concept, abstraction, or pattern that makes a specific material object intelligible. There are higher forms and lower forms according to the degree of abstraction or generality (e.g. pure math and applied math), and there are higher and lower entities within the physical realm, for example, a man and a picture of a man.

Two of Plato's famous analogies illustrate this hierarchy. *The divided line* represents a spectrum of being and knowledge, divided first into halves. The first division is between physical reality (known by sense experience), and formal reality (known by the intellect). The two further divisions are between images and physical objects in the lower half (known by sense experience) and between lower and higher forms in the higher half (known by respectively lower and higher levels of intellect).

The second analogy depicts a bizarre scenario with prisoners chained inside a cave, their heads held in a position so that they can see only a wall in front of them. Behind the prisoners, people parade back and forth while holding objects on their heads. Further behind the prisoners, a fire casts images of those objects onto the wall which fills the prisoners' entire field of vision. The analogy depicts people bound by chains of ignorance, facing a wall bearing images (the physical world) which they mistake for reality, but which are only imitations of the real things (the forms) located before the fire behind them. Only by breaking these chains and turning to gaze upon the objects themselves could these people recognize the wall for what it is, a fake, a poor copy of true Being. Likewise, only through exercise of the intellect and dialectic can we loose the fetters of our own ignorance to know true Being, the source of the shadowy experience of everyday life. Just as the initial glimpse of the actual cave objects, backlit by fire, is a painful shock, difficult to withstand (not to mention the eventual sight of the sun itself), so is the process of philosophical enlightenment an ordeal. It takes an adjustment of the eyes/mind to look comfortably upon the forms. But once they have been seen and known for what they are, the prospect of a descent to one's former place in the depths of common experience is intolerable.

In the third analogy, the Good, the source of all being and knowledge, is likened to the sun, the source of light and therefore vision itself. Just as the sun cannot itself be seen (since it is what makes vision itself possible), neither can the Good be known.

A simple example of the superiority of formal to physical reality can be seen in the form (idea) of a right triangle versus a wooden or plastic drafting triangle. The form of a right triangle (or of *right triangularity* as it were) has certain properties that are eternal. For example, the square of the hypotenuse is, has always been, and will always be equal to the sum of the squares of the other two sides. The sum of the interior angles is, has always been, and will always be one hundred and eighty degrees. And even if there never had been and never would be any physical triangle, what we have just said about triangularity would still be true. On the other hand, if we didn't know right triangularity, we would not recognize a drafting triangle for what it is, and in fact, it would not exist as a drafting triangle, but only as a piece of plastic (which in turn could exist or be known only in terms of what plastic is). Triangularity is eternal, drafting triangles only ephemeral and incomplete.

We understand or recognize circles, squares, lines and points without ever experiencing anything but approximations, and we recognize those approximations only in terms of the forms (concepts). Likewise, we do not experience perfect justice, piety, honor, or love, but we recognize and evaluate instances according to certain standards, certain forms.

# Aristotle



*predication*
*the four causes*
*the unmoved mover*
*infinite regress*


Whereas the Platonic worldview can be at least roughly apprehended in a single vision of metaphysical, epistemological, and axiological hierarchy, Aristotelian philosophy tends invariably towards labyrinthine analysis, breaking everything down and sorting out the parts.  For example, there are ten ways of *predicating* anything of (saying anything about) an object of knowledge. Primarily there is substance, which is what distinguishes an object from all other objects. The others are by reference to its quantity, quality, relation, place, time, position, having, affecting something else, and being affected. Thus, Cecil is large and green, one of only six sea monsters, at the bottom of the ocean, in a painfully contorted posture, sporting an underwater top hat, scaring all the water babies, and being pestered by a swarm of jellyfish. Aristotle also sets out all the rules for how to reason correctly (logic), and his *four "causes"* are to account for how anything is what it is. They are (1) the *material cause* (not surprisingly, whatever material the thing consists of), (2) the *efficient cause* (whatever agent brought the thing about), (3) the *formal cause* (whatever we recognize the thing to be – notably inseparable from the thing itself, unlike Plato's forms), and (4) the *final cause* (the purpose of the thing). Hence, the nail is "caused" by the iron that makes it up (material), the blacksmith's forging of the iron (efficient), the shape and the size (formal), and the purpose of holding the shoe on the horse (final).

And God, the *unmoved* (or *prime*) *mover*, is the only alternative to an *infinite regress of causation* (with any of the four causes), a notion Aristotle apparently thought too absurd to bother refuting. Take final causality: thing #1 exists to serve thing #2, which exists to serve thing #3, and so on. Aristotle thought that there would have to be some ultimate purpose to be served by the chain of servant things. To think otherwise would be like trying to explain a hanging chain's suspension in terms of each link's being held up by the one above it. The idea of a world which exists in its links of purpose to serve a single ultimate purpose is called *teleological*.

Aristotle was utterly catholic (meaning universal) in his interests, and his contributions to many diverse areas of knowledge were considered authoritative, beginning around the 11th century and continuing for centuries to follow. It was around the 11th century that the Church's preference for Aristotelian thought began to replace Plato's influence.

## Commentary: Either/Or

It has been suggested that you are born either a Platonist or an Aristotelian and that whichever you are, you will never change. Perhaps it is genetic. There is no independent party. No straddling of the metaphysical fence. No bi- or transphilosophicals. No hybrids, no combos, no best of both worlds.

Blow hot or cold.

PlatonistAristotelians are like CatDogs in their nonexistence. If you are a Platonist, the earth is your prison. A cave. If you are an Aristotelian, you are "down to earth." The Platonist is forever in an orbit of abstraction, while the Aristotelian maintains an immanence in the world. This life, for the Platonist, is a shadow, a procession of ghostly shapes, a gross approximation of the angelic realm. The Aristotelian accepts fully the worldliness of life and expects in return the world's full cooperation with the rules of reason.

The Platonist looks at the physical world and sees an obvious falling-short of the reality that glistens in the understanding and that is pure and eternal. The Platonist wonders how the Aristotelian can take experience for more than a dream, a shadow of Truth, even as Being shines through and upon the world, illuminating it for the mind, calling the mind upwards and out of its sensory confines.

The Aristotelian kicks a rock and feels being in the pain, feels the hardness of matter and wonders how the Platonist can be so numb to the brute reality of the material world. The form is *in* the thing, not removed, not existing on a higher plane. The form *needs* the thing, the Aristotelian insists, and who could not see that?

# The Medieval Period

## Introduction

*fideism*
*otherworldliness*
*hierarchy*
*Neoplatonism*

For the next fifteen centuries or so, at least within Western civilization, philosophy survived in something of a straightjacket, if not a coma, imposed by the Catholic Church. *Fideism* is a key term for the predominant mentality of the time, meaning that faith, rather than reason, is our only source for Truth, and more specifically, faith in the Church as founded by Christ through Peter, as stated inerrantly in Scripture, which of course was available mainly to the Church. Free exercise of reason was best kept to oneself.

Add to faith an abiding preoccupation with *otherworldliness*, the other world being heaven. Christ said, "My kingdom is not of this world," and thus were the faithful encouraged, by the Church, to forsake the here and now for the hereafter, earthly power and goods for spiritual reward, worldly worth for treasure in heaven, pleasures of the flesh for the sublimity of the soul, for though we may be *in* this world, we are not *of* this world. (Of course this adoptive listlessness by the masses accorded well with the upper ranks of Medieval society, namely the royalty/nobility and Catholic hierarchy, but more on this when we get to Marx and Hegel.)

A third influence on what passed for philosophy during much of the medieval period was the *hierarchical structure* of Church, society, and in fact the universe as it was seen. The classes of society ranged from the monarch at the top, followed by knights, nobles and higher clergy (which had its own hierarchy), then lower clergy, merchants and professionals in the middle, and peasants and serfs at the lowest rungs. In a cosmological context, the spiritual realm comprised God at the top, followed by the different choirs of angels, and in the physical realm were man (sort of an angel/beast), then animals, and then (following the Great Chain as it was later called) plants and minerals. Ontologically, the greater the spirit/body ratio, the higher the rank of existence.

Now, the philosophy of Plato clearly depicts a hierarchy of Being as well as knowledge, the superiority of the formal world over the physical corresponding nicely with the otherworldliness of Christianity. So whatever liberty philosophy had left under the authority of the Church, given the cleavage in metaphysics wrought by Plato and Aristotle, it was only a matter of course for the Church to favor Plato over Aristotle. And in fact, a number of minor players among the early Medieval intelligentsia are now referred to as *Neoplatonists* (Plotinus, Porphyry, et al).

# Saint Augustine

*crede ut intellegas*
*The City of God* and *Confessions*
*divine omniscience vs. free will*
*evil as privation*
*voluntarism*
*si fallor sum*

Saint Augustine of Hippo, a Christian Platonist foremost and most approved by the Church, managed to negotiate around the fideism of the day, in large part by the preface *crede ut intellegas* (believe in order to understand), thus preserving the ultimacy of faith as the basis for belief while still allowing for the exercise of reason with that caveat.

In addition to his well-known *Confessions* (autobiographical), Augustine's *City of God* is considered to be the first significant philosophy of history; that is, the first attempt to account for history as following a pattern according to identifiable principles, specifically God's plan for the Jews.

And speaking of God's relationship with events in time, Augustine is known for facing head-on the perceived problem of God's omnipotence vis-à-vis our freedom of choice. That is, if God knows beforehand what our choice will be, then how is it free? As a solution, Augustine pointed out that God, being eternal, does not exist in time, and thus there is no before or after to His omniscience. And a corollary to God's atemporal existence is that time does not exist at the level of the fully real (cf modern physics).

One clear case of Augustine's applying Plato's hierarchical metaphysics to Christian theology has to do with the solution to the problem of evil, given an all-good and omnipotent God. How and why, the question runs, would God allow, much less cause, evil to exist if He is all about Good? Augustine's answer is that evil doesn't actually exist, but rather is the *privation of good* and therefore of being itself. Evil is misperceived as real and often mistaken for good, but like the projections of images on Plato's cave wall, evil is distant from God and therefore insubstantial.

Having dealt with both the problems of free will and the apparent existence of evil, Augustine is faced with the problem of both combined: if God loves us, why would He allow us to risk choosing evil (the unreal) over good (the real)? The answer is that human freedom is worth the risk of making a wrong choice.

Just as, for Plato, truth has its source in goodness (the hierarchy of knowledge having its source in the Good), Augustine saw all truth as the result of God's will. This belief is called *voluntarism*. Also, like Plato, Augustine saw our ability to know timeless truths (such as mathematical ones) as proof of our immortal or eternal souls.

Finally, all the Platonism in Augustine's work notwithstanding, and even within the theological straightjacket of the day, one insight in particular places Augustine centuries ahead of his time, and that is his refutation of thoroughgoing skepticism. At least since the second century A.D., this ghost of doubt has lurked like waiting death in the background of philosophers' attempts to know. Is truth after all knowable? Or is belief more of an attitude, determined less by the object of belief than by the believer? How do we know that we know? Mistakes happen, even about things that seem most certain. Is there any belief at all that is exempt from the possibility of error? Well, reasoned Augustine, even if I err, I know at least that I exist. This simple statement, *si fallor, sum*, if I err, I exist, might have shone brighter in the history of philosophy if there had been any prominent skeptics to silence at the time. But in the age of fideism, the significance of Augustine's insight was largely lost in the shadow of faith.

### Commentary: On Evil

For Parmenides the absence of being was unthinkable and therefore impossible. Implications of this point were that unity and permanence were essential qualities of being, the apparent world, in all its whirling spectacle, a mere phantasm. Plato made explicit the connection between being and goodness in his theory of forms. Thus for Plato, the less good something was, the less real. And Augustine insisted repeatedly on the point that "that which we call evil [is] but the absence of good" (*Enchiridion*).

As a *Christian Platonist*, Augustine found in Plato's hierarchy a convenient solution to the problem of reconciling the existence of evil with God's omnipotence and goodness: evil is simply not real. (Just as cold is not really something, only the absence of heat?) On the other hand, as is commonly experienced and often remarked, it is sometimes easier to believe in evil than to believe in God. In fact, the evil in the world can seem to be the manifestation of an actual force, sentient, intentional. The myth of Satan is not about the absence of good. Darkness, the absence of light, still has its prince, a powerful, conniving force.

And just as Thomas of Aquinas will argue from the design of the world that there must be a God, who has not wondered if there is some dark manipulation of narrative to bring out the worst in us? History and literature are full of largely decent men and women who, by an apparent conspiracy of circumstances, succumb to their inevitable flaws. As Hamlet says of them,

Their virtues else — be they as pure as grace,
As infinite as man may undergo —
Shall in the general censure take corruption
From that particular fault. The dram of e'il
Doth all the noble substance often dout
To his own scandal.

Look at Oedipus. Look at Macbeth. Read *Eichmann in Jerusalem*.

So what is evil? The mere privation of good or something real, a fallen power, a malevolent force, a dark side of Being itself?

# The Scholastic Period



*Anselm's ontological proof of God's existence*
*Occam's razor*
*Saint Thomas of Aquinas (separate section)*

Along about the 11th century, with the advent of *scholasticism*, the darkness of the so-called Dark Ages began to wane as the primacy of faith gave way, however gradually, to the exercise of reason. Slowly the fixation on the hereafter conceded to a growing recognition of the here-and-now. Of the two great grandsires of philosophy, Aristotle assumed the status of most favored, which Plato had held for a millennium. Theologians acquired a taste for debate. Abelard's *Sic et Non (Yes and No)* exemplified the sort of dialectical reasoning that was fashionable at the time.

Saint Anselm of Canterbury dropped something of a philosophical bombshell known now as the first ontological proof of God. A rough paraphrase runs as follows: Imagine or conceive of that than which nothing greater can be conceived; i.e., a perfect being. If the object of this conception did not exist, it would not be a perfect being (i.e., it would not be that than which nothing greater can be conceived, since a being that exists is clearly greater than one that doesn't). The object of this conception necessarily exists. Hence, God exists.

In the unlikely event that the reader was an atheist before reading this and has suddenly found, for example, a reason to go on living, fine. Or if, like many of the theologians of Anselm's day, the reader feels that it is an act of hubris to venture by reason where faith alone is granted passage as a gift from the Almighty, then that is fine too. But the point is, does it make sense to talk about an essence that entails existence? Is there anything which, by virtue of its being understandable (knowable for what it is as opposed to something else) must necessarily exist? Is there anything which contains the very grounds (cause) of its own existence?

Also during this time, William of Occam authored a famous dictum which most scientists assume as a matter of course. "It is vain to do with more what can be done with less," or to apply the same principle to a paraphrase, the simplest explanation is the best. This principle is known as Occam's razor.

# Thomas of Aquinas

*natural vs. revealed theology*
*five proofs of God's existence (cosmological, cosmic*
*harmony, and standards of value)*
*four causes*

Before the advent of the Renaissance and its complete recovery from the intellectual sluggishness of the Middle Ages, Saint Thomas of Aquinas married philosophy and theology in one comprehensive, Church-approved system, titled *Summa Theologia*, which together with *Summa Contra Gentiles*, became the official philosophy of the Church.

Thomist theology is considered *natural* as opposed to *revealed* because it is grounded in reason and observation of nature rather than exclusively in revelation. Also, in true Aristotelian style, Thomas's writings are detailed, painstaking, and sweeping and do not lend themselves to summary. However, his approach to one special topic well exemplifies Aristotle's influence and natural theology's basis in reason and observation of nature. That topic has to do with God's existence, of which Thomas proposed five proofs. The first three, known collectively as the *cosmological proofs*, are but subtle variations on the fundamental problem of the *infinite regress*, which is taken straight out of the Aristotelian playbook. The other two, based on the *harmony in nature* and on *standards of value,* illustrate the natural theologian's inference from nature to the divine.

Now, as for the cosmological proofs, we may remember that Aristotle divided causation into four types: (1) material, (2) efficient, (3) formal, and (4) final. And since everything must have a cause, that cause must itself be caused, and that cause must be caused, and so on *ad infinitum,* unless there is some ultimate cause, which Aristotle called the *prime mover.* Thomas's cosmological proofs of God's existence are not appreciably different in their form, only in their categorization of links of dependency (or purpose). Thomas divided these links into (1) *movement,* (2) *cause,* and (3) *contingency.*

> (1) Everything that moves is moved by the movement of something, which in turn must be moved by the movement of something, and so on.
>
> (2) Every event must be caused by an event, and so on.
>
> (3) Everything is contingent upon something else, and so on.

Obviously, the *so on* in all three cases would amount to an infinite regress unless some self-moved mover, self-caused cause, and ultimately independent Being existed. Hence, God exists.

Another proof, based on *perfect harmony* in nature, is similar to the idea of *intelligent design* meant to counter the teaching of evolution in the schools. The complexity and order of the world seem too great to be the result of mere chance; hence, there must be some ordering principle behind nature; hence, God exists.

The fifth proof actually recalls Plato's arguments regarding the forms as standards by which we recognize objects, especially as good or poor specimens. For anything to be good or better than another, there must be some standard of goodness – perfection – and God is the only candidate for the position.

The ghost of fideism continued to haunt philosophy through the Renaissance and even into the Enlightenment, but the changes in methodology that started with scholasticism gained validation with Thomas and led ultimately to the rebirth of learning.

## Commentary: On an Implied God

We saw that the beginning of philosophy was the beginning of the end of our communion with the gods via nature. First water, then the *apeiron*, then air, and so on, all lifeless *stuff*, all wore away at the divinely animated world. Then Parmenides gave us the big changeless One Being, dismissing vibrant, active nature as one would a fanciful dream. (Such a Being is to life as death is to life, and this will not be the last time reason collides with vitality itself.) Plato was less reductive than the Presocratics in his hierarchical account in which the world at least reflected the ideal, but then came the Church, whereby a line was drawn between the worldly and the otherworldly, the former debased for its very materiality, while the latter, even in its separateness and remoteness, replaced the earth as our true home, thus making us aliens where we live.

So as scholasticism provides a transition from the Middle Ages to the Renaissance, and philosophical reasoning is given a freer rein, Saints Anselm and Thomas set out to construct logical proofs of God's existence. For Anselm, God is "that than which nothing greater can be conceived." For Thomas, God is (among other things of course) the only alternative to the absurdity of an infinite regress.

Not to disparage logical proofs of God's existence, but in thinking of God in those terms, it wouldn't hurt to remember the loss that accrued with the proposition that everything is water.

Happily, with the coming of the Renaissance, the natural theology of scholasticism evolved into a full-blown reverence for creation itself, and the otherworldliness of the past thirteen centuries gave way to a somewhat freer exercise of human resourcefulness and creativity.

# The Renaissance

*The Copernican Revolution*
*heliocentric vs. geocentric universe*
*Galileo's telescope*
*humanism*
*Martin Luther and the Protestant Reformation*
*Newton's Principia Mathematica*
*Hobbes's The Leviathan*

So yes, the Renaissance was a birth -- a rebirth (of learning), as the word means -- not without its labor pains. The Church did not take kindly to the fashion of eyeing the world through the lens of reason and sensory observation. For example, touting *Copernicus's claim that the earth was not the center of the universe* could get you burned at the stake, as Bruno, a Dominican friar, found out the hard way. Vanini and others met similar ends for countering the Church's view on nature and the cosmos, and Galileo himself was sentenced to life imprisonment (at his home) by concurring with *Copernicus's claim that the sun was central in the heavens, not the earth.*

Still, the Renaissance was a time of inexorable development toward a more worldly worldview and away from the controlling influence by an increasingly corrupt and sidelined Church. Reason and observation moved in uneven supersession of scripture and the Pope in shaping the view of nature and the cosmos. For this new worldliness, the cultural movement was guided by a constellation of wealth, education, capitalist leanings, and political influence. *Humanism, the belief that humanity was capable of fulfillment by its own devices,* budded with the likes of Thomas More and his emphasis on reason. *Martin Luther, the central figure in the Protestant Reformation, insisted that individual conscience was the ultimate basis for faith, not the Church.* And the visual arts shifted focus from a mere religious illustration to the human body and worldly beauty (e.g. da Vinci and Michelangelo.)

The aforementioned claim by Copernicus that the sun, not the earth, was the center of the universe, though largely ignored until after his death, had a huge effect in altering humankind's view of itself in relation to the world and to God, so huge that the phrase *Copernican Revolution is still used as a metaphor for any large-scale change in the way of viewing something* (but more frequently referred to today as a *paradigm shift*). For its entire history, the *Church had held to the Egyptian astronomer Ptolemy's view that the universe was earth-centered, or geocentric,* since Ptolemy's view accorded with the Bible. Not since Thales had replaced a man/god with water had there been such a relegation of man as when Copernicus removed him from the center of creation. Oddly enough, it was not until Galileo confirmed Copernican theory, with the use of his telescope, that the uproar over *heliocentrism (placing the sun at the center)* began.

And if Copernicus can be compared to Thales, Isaac Newton can be fairly compared to Aristotle. Newton's *Principia Mathematica combined mathematics, astronomy, and physics of the day to provide a comprehensive mechanistic account of the universe.*

Of course it was inevitable that someone (*Thomas Hobbes*) would write a book (*The Leviathan*) in which similarly *mechanistic principles would be applied to an account of the human body, mind, and society*, thus anticipating the likes of Darwin, Freud, and Marx respectively.

## Commentary: "On the Shore of the Wide World"

Copernicus published *On the Revolutions of the Celestial Spheres* in 1543, putting forth a heliocentric view of the universe to replace Ptolemy's geocentric view. After Copernicus's death, Galileo, for his public agreement with Copernicus, was sentenced to house arrest for life, while others were burned at the stake for the same public profession. Mankind, the Church insisted, is at the center of creation. Centuries later, John Keats would write the poem "When I Have Fears That I May Cease to Be," listing in vain and florid detail the loss that too early a death would bring to himself and the world. The poem concludes, " — then on the shore / Of the wide world I stand, and think / Till love and fame to nothingness do sink."

Standing on that shore, we now know that the world is a miniscule speck of mostly iron and silicon, spinning its little circles around an average-size star, one of one hundred billion to four hundred billion stars in an average-size galaxy, itself one of possibly two trillion galaxies, in the *observed* universe, which incidentally has no "center," a fact which defies our intuitions of space and time, intuitions which have little if any correlation with the space/time fabric, a fabric that is likely not even fundamental but emergent, having emerged from something even more fundamental some 13.8 billion years ago.

So if you are banking on your location in the universe as a sign of prominence in God's eyes, then bless your heart, but it seems there might be more to the idea as a metaphor than as a literal fact. If the universe is not heliocentric, then mightn't it still be somehow *anthropocentric*? That is, mightn't humankind be central in terms of something more meaningful than astronomy, perhaps something more metaphysical than physical?

In fact, once philosophy resumes fully charged and independent of theology, it does so with nothing more than the indubitable fact of oneself. The self becomes the real center, the ultimate source, of both metaphysics and physics.

## The Enlightenment

Following the Renaissance, the period of Western history known variously as *the Enlightenment, the Age of Reason,* and *the Neoclassical Period* began to take shape in an intellectual environment determined largely by three conflicting factors. First, the Church was at least a lingering authority to be reckoned with. Second, reason and empirical observation were recommending themselves more and more as bases for knowledge. And third, Michel de Montaigne, on rediscovering the writings of Sextus Empiricus (a second century philosopher) added to the whole intellectual stew some compelling arguments for a thoroughgoing philosophical *skepticism*; that is, the position that infallible knowledge is simply not possible. Montaigne pointed out, for example, that no matter how certain our claim to knowledge seems to be, countless others have felt equally certain, only to be proved wrong. Thus it was the promise of reason vs. the shadow of doubt that became the battle of the philosophical giants of the time, with the Church somehow to be accommodated.

As stated above, reason and empirical observation had become increasingly convincing methods in the pursuit of knowledge, but which was to hold the ultimate sway? The old Greek opposition of understanding vs. experience reappeared in the Enlightenment as two opposing schools of thought, known respectively as *(continental) rationalism* and *(British) empiricism.*

The three principal icons of continental rationalism are Descartes, Leibniz, and Spinoza. Of the British empiricists, Locke, Berkeley, and Hume are the chief players.

# The Rationalists



René Descartes took seriously both the prospect of knowing reality by our own devices –– knowing it as certainly as we know that $2 + 2 = 4$ –– and the ultimate philosophical doubt that had surfaced with the revival of skepticism. Resolving to settle the issue for good, he decided to extend a methodological, hyperbolic doubt as far as it would go (no matter how strange or odd it might seem to doubt the existence of the physical world), but with the understanding that if anything were to remain absolutely indubitable, then there would be his "Archimedean point" of absolute certainty on which to base all of philosophy.

Thus, *Meditations on First Philosophy* proceeds, first, with a *progressive methodological doubt*, beginning with the suspicion of appearance as being tricks of perspective. (Is that really a cat sitting over there in the fog or an oddly shaped stump?) Next he wonders about the very existence of physical objects. (Am I only dreaming? Is life but a dream?) Finally, shifting to an indirect, or *second order doubt*, he subjects simple mathematical truths to another type of scrutiny. Even though one cannot directly doubt that 2 + 2 = 4, one can still entertain the prospect that an "evil genius" has somehow distorted one's very faculty of perception such that even what is directly indubitable is nevertheless false, perceived as it were through the bent lens of the mind. And with that hypothesis, Descartes is satisfied to have found the limit of doubt.

Next (in the 2nd Meditation) Descartes wonders whether anything remains, anything that has escaped even the second order doubt by the evil genius hypothesis. And here he arrives at the sought-after Archimedean point of support for modern philosophy: the *cogito*. In the act of doubting, or of simply thinking, he finds certainty of his own existence, a certainty invulnerable even to deception by an evil genius, for even being deceived requires existence. The phrase *I think; therefore, I am* (*cogito; ergo, sum*), while not used in the *Meditations* themselves, serves as a methodological commencement for many philosophers up through the twentieth century. It should be noted that this initial, radically limited certainty is referred to as solipsism, meaning that for all one knows for certain, the self could be the only existing entity in the universe.

And for Descartes, the *cogito* leads directly to the certain awareness of his own imperfection, an idea which would not be possible without at least the idea of perfection, which could not have its source in an imperfect being. Hence, there must be some perfect Being (God), which exists as the source of his idea of perfection. (The more detailed formulation of this argument is known as Descartes's *ontological proof of God's existence*.)

Next comes a decreasingly convincing series of reasonings in which Descartes demonstrates how to avoid error and then restores believability to the material world.

Finally and famously comes what is known as *Cartesian dualism*; that is, the position that body and mind are separate entities. Descartes's argument is two-fold: the first part is based upon the fact that body and mind can be conceived separately, and the second has to do with that fact that while the body is divisible, the mind is not. Descartes concludes that body and mind, while separate and distinct, must be divinely correlated. Thus hoping to reconcile the two conflicting authorities of science and the Church, he allows that while science should be free to express its findings regarding the body, the mind remains under the purview of the Church.

Next of the three main continental rationalists, Spinoza is best known for his magnum opus, the *Ethics*, a tedious read (to put it mildly). One may or may not agree with his arguments, but few would deny the historical significance of its method, which follows the form of geometric proofs. He begins with a set of definitions and a set of axioms and proceeds to construct a chain of proofs about the nature of God and man, thus bringing to philosophical method the same perceived certitude as in mathematics.

And then there is Leibniz, known more (fairly or unfairly) as the butt of a famous joke than for whatever profundity his work may contain. The joke is in Voltaire's novel *Candide: or the Optimist*, a dark satire of the pretentious loftiness of philosophy, especially the philosophical optimism of Voltaire's time and its disconnect with the conditions in the real world. The character of Professor Pangloss is immediately recognizable as a parody of Leibniz and his well-known claim that ours is the *"best of all possible worlds."*

## Commentary: The Ghost in the Machine

It is a strange thought that that very thought might be a mere physical process in the brain, an almost inconceivably complicated event in which millions of neurons linked in a cerebral network of stupendous complexity fire off signals through neural tracts, electrical impulses, molecular communication through intricate paths, all to produce a fleeting phenomenon known commonly as a "thought." And yet a great many scientists and philosophers insist that the "mind" or "consciousness" is reducible to just such a mechanistic process.

Of course many others think not. They think the mind is of a whole different order of reality from the body, that consciousness will never be accounted for by the same mechanistic principles used to explain the physical world.

Still a third group of highly reputable scientists believe that the universe itself is in some important sense *conscious*. In a converse of the materialists' view, some quantum physicists (for example) believe that on the deepest level, material is reducible to something like mind.

But only the second group are stuck with the problem, once having accepted Descartes's mind/body split, of explaining how the two are related. No dualist would deny that there is some mysterious coordination between the two (fingers wiggle at mind's will). Even if it's God Who somehow links the pair (maybe in the pineal gland, as Descartes suggested, if only half seriously), Gilbert Ryle's derisive description of Cartesian dualism as the "ghost in the machine" persists to this day.

Now, to elevate the language slightly, and to place the question among contemporary concerns, if *mind* equals *soul* (as it seems to have for Descartes) at what point in the body's embryonic development does the soul enter? Consciousness? And at what point does the soul depart? Brain death?

But there is a fourth view of the mind/body problem that would accept the two components but deny the split; that is, we occupy a rather fraught place on the Chain of Being, neither angel nor beast but something in between, straddling the realms of the physical and the spiritual. Alexander Pope puts it wonderfully in "An Essay on Man." We are, he says,

> Plac'd on this isthmus of a middle state,
> A being darkly wise, and rudely great:
> With too much knowledge for the sceptic side,
> With too much weakness for the stoic's pride,
> He hangs between; in doubt to act, or rest;
> In doubt to deem himself a god, or beast;
> In doubt his mind or body to prefer;
> Born but to die, and reas'ning but to err;
> Alike in ignorance, his reason such,
> Whether he thinks too little, or too much:
> Chaos of thought and passion, all confus'd;
> Still by himself abus'd, or disabus'd;
> Created half to rise, and half to fall;
> Great lord of all things, yet a prey to all;
> Sole judge of truth, in endless error hurl'd:
> The glory, jest, and riddle of the world!

# The Empiricists



Meanwhile across the English Channel, the British (empiricists) sought a foundation for certainty in the immediate sensory content of consciousness. Experience via the five sensory modes cannot be denied, they reasoned, though it is for philosophy to determine what relationship this experience bears to any world outside the mind.

The primacy of experience as the source of knowledge is classically expressed in John Locke's description of the mind at birth as a *tabula rasa*, or blank slate. Locke summarily rejected the Platonic notion of innate ideas, arguing that all mental contents are combinations of sensations and reflections (remembering, abstracting, etc.). Objects in the world outside the mind, he reasoned, have three types of qualities: (1) primary, those inhering in the object, such as shape, weight, etc., (2) secondary, the power to produce sensations in us, and (3) tertiary, the power to affect other objects.

Of course it didn't take much of a leap for someone, George Berkeley, to point out, in good Cartesian fashion, that if sensations are mental (internal to the mind) and are the ultimate basis for knowledge, there is no logical basis for knowledge of objects external to the mind, including whether they exist at all. So while he is an empiricist, he is also an *immaterialist*, stating famously that *esse est percipi* (*to be is to be perceived*). There are no unknown substrates out there, and if there were, we could never know them. But if there is no material out there corresponding to our mentally lived world, then how is the great totality of our perceptions orchestrated into such a coherent arrangement, and if there are no secondary qualities of material objects, then what is the cause of our sensation? God, Berkeley says, is the great conductor of experience. God, in His omnipotence, has no need for a material medium. All reality is spiritual. And science, Berkeley says, is the exploration of the mind of God.

Is it any wonder then that once Bishop Berkeley (yes, an Anglican bishop) dispensed with the material world as the source of knowledge – had identified God Himself exclusively as the direct fabricator of the grand interplay of perceptions, and had thus hung a whole epistemology on the ghostly object of faith – that David Hume, a man of far less reverence and with a mind like a dagger, would step in to wreak havoc on both empiricism's and rationalism's professed grasp on the nature of reality? David Hume, a so-called "wrecking ball" of a philosopher, targeted not only God and the physical world to expose as philosophical fictions but also the very self that gave Descartes his Archimedean point of certainty. Other casualties included the concept of cause and effect and any but the most cynical view of morality itself.

Hume accepts the premise of the empiricists that experience (in the traditional philosophical sense) is the ultimate source of mental contents, calling these most fundamental objects of awareness *impressions*. (Ideas, he says, are copies of impressions.) His next point is crucial to the threatened unraveling of all claims to certainty by both the rationalists and the empiricists. Hume observes that all impressions and ideas are "*distinct and separable*." In other words, there is no "*necessary connection*" between any two of them. Now, the whole concept of causation entails a necessary connection between the effect and the cause. But since our knowledge of each is only in terms of impressions, which are themselves distinct and separable, then we cannot know that any two phenomena are causally connected. The misconstrual comes from the "*constant conjunction*" of certain pairs of familiar impressions. It is convenient to believe in cause and effect, just as it is convenient to believe in God and the self, although all three beliefs are ultimately unsupported by impressions and are therefore irrational.

## Commentary: Monster

By many accounts, Hume in the flesh was less than charming. He wore an expression easily taken as moronic, and the word "corpulent" is often used regarding his physique. Add to all this his malevolent seeming delight in the wholesale destruction of the philosophical edifices of the day, and he comes across as something of a monster. Targeting God, morality, the self, the physical world, and the very concept of causality, undermining them all at least for a while, he finally led himself into an abyss of depression, untethered and lost. Until he recovered, revived by celebrity.

One imagines Hume as kind of a Grendel, a shadow of doubt that follows faith, the dark self, cackling in the background of our noble discourse in pursuit of truth. James Boswell reports that even on his death bed, Hume was dismissive and "impolite" on the subjects of God, the soul, and the afterlife.

If nothing else, Hume was a speed bump to the headlong charge of both rationalist and empiricist overconfidence and naïve optimism. No one doubts Hume's genius, and his eloquence is a pleasure in its own right. But most importantly, Hume's devastating critique of the highest claims to knowledge set the perfect stage for the Kantian revolution to follow, a true paradigm shift in how to think about thought itself.

# Kant

*The Kantian Revolution*
*a posteriori*
*a priori*
*analytic judgements*
*synthetic judgements*
*transcendental search*
*categories of the intuition*
*categories of the understanding*
*transcendental unity of apperception*
*transcendental imagination*
*phenomena*
*noumena*
*hypothetical imperatives*
*categorical imperatives*
*THE categorical imperative*

So to review, Locke, Berkeley, and Hume all agree on the certainty of immediate sensory contents of the mind (such as the present experience of a vile odor). But what Hume showed empiricism can't account for is the coherent connectedness of sensation into an apparent world.

Rationalism, on the other hand, seeks to go beyond sensory experience in order to obtain knowledge of reality and with the same certainty afforded in mathematics. But the question lingers following Descartes's "evil genius" hypothesis: Is the mind itself structured for access to ultimate truth, or is the very faculty for thought something like a bent lens through which the light of truth is inevitably distorted? To answer that question, what is needed is a critique of reason itself to determine once and for all whether reason is equipped to know truth, specifically metaphysical truth. Thus, in writing his *Critique of Pure Reason*, (in what is known as the Kantian Copernican revolution, or simply the *Kantian revolution*), Immanuel Kant effected a kind of synthesis of empiricist and rationalist principles to show how the world is both a construct and object of knowledge.

## Kant's *Critique of Pure Reason*: an Ultra Concise Sketch

To begin, Kant distinguishes between two kinds of knowledge corresponding to the two schools of philosophy prominent in his time.

Knowledge based on experience (empirical) is *a posteriori*; that is, after or post experience. An example would be the knowledge that that cat is unfriendly.

*A priori* refers to knowledge that is independent of, before, or prior to, experience. *A priori* knowledge is of what is *necessarily* and *universally* true. An example would be that in a right triangle, the square of the hypotenuse is equal to the sum of the squares of the other two sides. One does not base such knowledge on experience with individual triangles. This is knowledge of a property of any right triangle anywhere and at any time, and it is impossible for it to be false of any right triangle.

Next, Kant distinguishes between two types of judgement, *analytic* and *synthetic*. An *analytic judgement* is derived from an analysis of the concept contained in the grammatical subject. Thus an analytic judgement is only *explicative*. For example, in the sentence "all quadrupeds have legs," the predicate identifies one quality included in the concept of a quadruped. Analytic judgements provide no new information about the subject, only an analysis of its meaning.

*Synthetic judgements*, on the other hand, add information to all the information contained in the subject itself. In other words, synthetic judgements are truly informative as opposed to merely explicative. For example, "All politicians are liars," whether true or false, is a synthetic judgement because lying is not part of the concept of a politician.

Now, after distinguishing between two types of knowledge and between two types of judgement, Kant lays out four different combinations of types of knowledge with types of judgement.

(1) *Analytic a posteriori* judgements cannot arise, since the mere analysis of a concept would not need any basis in experience.

(2) *Synthetic a posteriori* judgements are based on experience and report new information about the concept in the subject. These judgements tend to be of little metaphysical significance. "Cats are hard to train" or "Louise has fleas," while informative about cats or Louise, are unremarkable as forms of judgements.

(3) *Analytic a priori* judgements are matters of certainty, independent of experience, but add no information beyond what is contained in the concept in the grammatical subject. "All effects have causes," for example, is necessarily and universally true, but yields no new information about effects since it simply draws on the concept – the definition – of "effect" as grounds for its truth.

(4) *Synthetic a priori* judgements are, to put it mildly, central to Kant's critique. These judgements state what is necessarily and universally true, with absolute certainty, and are totally independent of experience. Furthermore, they are truly informative in that they tell us something

that cannot be derived from an analysis of the concept contained in the subject. We know, for example, that *all events have causes* (as distinct from *all effects have causes*), even though this knowledge is not derived from experience, nor is the predicate (*have causes*) derived from an analysis of the subject. The judgement is universally and necessarily true. How, then, do we know it? What are the grounds for *synthetic a priori judgements*?

Kant's critique can be read as a *transcendental search* for the grounds for *synthetic a priori judgements*. *Transcendental* here refers to a certain self-consciousness that the mind adopts in order to observe and analyze itself in the process of knowing. In so doing, the mind is able to sort out the various structures that make it up and thus determine how it functions.

Two of these structures, *space* and *time*, Kant calls *categories of the intuition*. Consider the role of space and time in making experience possible. Try to imagine the world without them. You simply can't. But does that mean that space and time necessarily inhere in the world we perceive or that space and time inhere in our faculty for perceiving the world? (Hint: When we speak of seeing the world through rose-colored glasses, what we mean is that the inability to see the world as anything other than rose-colored means that it's the observer's glasses that are tinted, not the world that is rosy.)

Now, while the categories of intuition are conditions for sensory experience, another set of categories consists of conditions for understanding that experience as the experience of objects known conceptually. Kant's deduction of the *categories of the understanding* is tedious and arduous. So suffice it here to supply the table of the categories and then focus on one to illustrate their role in the formation of *synthetic a priori judgements.*

*Categories of the Understanding*

| OF QUANTITY | OF RELATION |
|:---:|:---:|
| unity | inherence |
| plurality | causality |
| totality | correlation |
| OF QUALITY | OF MODALITY |
| reality | possibility |
| negation | necessity |
| limitation | contingency |

The point is that these categories are structures of the mind that knows, the shape of the lens, the conditions of knowledge, or if you like, impositions on the possibility of experience. They are the way objects are conceptually formed out of the sensations present.

So back to the question of how *synthetic a priori judgements* are formed (for example, the judgement that *all events have causes*), it is necessarily in terms of the mind's structures (for example, *causality*) that an event can be recognized as an event. An uncaused event is simply inconceivable.

Knowledge of the world is a process of drawing from the categories of intuition and understanding to supply a connectedness among the totality of sensations. The agent of organization is what Kant calls the *transcendental unity of apperception*; that is, the mind's notion of itself as a self, a lasting unity of consciousness. In applying the categories, the agent has a degree of freedom for creativity, for which the *transcendental imagination* comes into play (an idea of which the romantic poets made a great deal, placing the imagination on a more transcendent plain than reason itself).

Kant calls the world as constructed by the mind the world of *phenomena*. He allows that there might be some *noumena*, or world in itself (he uses the German *Ding an sich*, or in English, the *thing in itself*) which the categories would not accommodate, but if so, he insists, we can never know anything about it, even whether it exists. The world as we know it is constructed purely for the possibility of experience. And metaphysics, he insists, is a pipe dream.

Here are the essential terms introduced above, used in a single sentence, to show at least how they relate to one another: The *transcendental unity of apperception* enlists the *transcendental imagination* in applying the *categories of intuition* and the *categories of the understanding* to the sensory manifold in order to render a world of *phenomena*.

But if Kant's insistence on the futility of metaphysics was absolute, he was equally unbending in his belief in a morality based on dispassionate reasoning and admitting of no exceptions. In his *Critique of Practical Reasoning*, he argues that moral imperatives must be categorical; otherwise, moral reasoning devolves into a morass of hypotheticals.

Not surprisingly, Kant begins his critique by distinguishing between two types of imperatives: hypothetical and categorical. *Hypothetical imperatives* are relative to a specific situation (a morality known more recently as *ethical relativism*). To accomplish that, do this. In a situation of personal gain vs. personal integrity, tell the truth. But when the welfare of others is at stake, it is permissible to lie. The problem with a morality based on hypothetical imperatives is that they provide no ultimate end or good to be accomplished – no final basis. *Categorical imperatives*, on the other hand, are absolute. Do this. Do not break promises. Period. Regardless of the circumstances. Of course, the problem with categorical imperatives is that under extenuating circumstances, the negative consequences may far outweigh the virtue of adherence to a categorical maxim. A terrorist has planted a bomb somewhere under Manhattan. I gain his trust and promise not to tell anyone if he tells me its location. He tells me. So do I stick to the categorical imperative not to break promises, or do I save Manhattan? Kant insisted that a categorical imperative is categorical and as such has no exceptions. Otherwise, we fall into a regress of aims (those things for the sake of which we act) and as with causality, that way lies absurdity.

So what imperatives are we to consider categorical? What are we to do? Kant's answer was that all categorical imperatives are derivatives of one, an imperative based on the universal character of reason itself: *Act only on that maxim whereby you can at the same time will that it should be universal law.*

## Commentary: This World, Right Here

Nowadays it is widely believed that space and time are two sides of the same coin, that time is a fourth dimension, and that neither is fundamental but rather emergent from something more basic, possibly something having to do with quantum entanglement. It is known that spacetime is not uniform, but warped as the gravity of mass, and that inside a black hole, time ends. Apparently space, time, everything to which the laws of physics apply, and maybe the laws themselves had a beginning, the issuance of the universe itself from a singularity, not *before* time, as the phrase makes no sense, but under conditions that are not spatiotemporal.

Regarding the necessity of causality for any event, an attendant belief is that if you subject two identical entities to identical conditions, the entities will react identically. Not true on the quantum level. There it's all about probability, the collapse of the probability wave coincident with being observed.

So now, slogging one's way through Kant's language, one has to wonder whether some of his points about (for example) space and time as categories of the intuition are downright moot in the light of recent science. Here it is worth remembering that the Copernican Revolution was no less revolutionary for the misplacement of the sun in the universe. The true impact was from the removal of the earth from the center. The impact of the Kantian Revolution is that the structure of the world as we see it is the result of the structure of our mind. In knowing the world, we in effect place it in space and time as we intuit them. And science – even quantum physics and general relativity – is not metaphysics. Kant's aim was to discover whether pure reason is adequate to determine metaphysical truths – truths about God, the soul, and such like. His conclusion is that it is not. Reason is for the experience of this world, right here.

# Hegel



*Geist*
*dialectical idealism*
*thesis/antithesis/synthesis*
*master-slave relationship*

In a sense, Hegel shared Kant's view of the world as a construct by the mind that perceives it, but Hegel would have nothing of the Kantian distinction between *phenomena* and (even the possibility of) *noumena.* In Hegel's own words, "What is real is rational, and what is rational is real." Furthermore, whereas Kant analyzed reason according to permanent structures in the individual's mind, Hegel saw these structures as fluid components of an organic, cosmic mind, or *Geist* that develops through history towards the goal of ultimate self-realization. For Hegel, truth itself changes as *Geist* grows like a tree, shedding old branches (of truth) as new ones grow. *Geist* (variously translated as *spirit, God, ghost,* and *mind*) develops through history by a process of *dialectical idealism, idealism* because *Geist* is idea, and *dialectical* because of the process of opposites generating syntheses.

For example, we might think of the 1950s in the United States as representing an idea (or set of ideas) about how to live. The times were clean-cut, wool-sweatered, patriarchal (as in *Father Knows Best*), and racially segregated. Everybody knew their place, and kids were free to roam the neighborhood without fear of predation. This worked just fine until women and blacks got sick of the oppression, the war in Vietnam led to a radical distrust of government and the establishment in general, the pill became a thing, and sex, drugs, and rock and roll became something of a morality (or as Timothy Leary put it, "Turn on, tune in, drop out.") Thus the 1960s became something of an *antithesis* of the 1950s. But as liberating as the 1960s were, the lifestyle was ultimately incompatible with the responsibilities that come with living a life. Still, some lessons were learned from the rebellion, lessons about civil rights, the dangers of certain varieties of uptightness, and probably the importance of personal hygiene. Thus in the 1970s, as rock and roll gave way to disco, tie dye to the pinstripe power suit, and LSD to cocaine in the executive restroom, and racism and sexism were at least tempered under the watch of affirmative action and *Ms.* magazine, a *synthesis* was formed of the cultures of the 1950s and 1960s.

Another instance of this dialectical process occurs as we are raised by our parents according to a certain set of values, which we hold to as a morality, believing them sound until we reach the age of twelve or thirteen when in a youthful rebellion we become the antithesis of the very selves our parents tried to mold. Then we have our own children and we come to realize that our parents might have gotten a few things right after all, although not everything. And so we raise our own children according to a synthesis of our parents' values and our own teenage rebellion, and the process continues as before.

History, according to Hegel, is a brutal warring of opposites, a "slaughter bench," in which *Geist* passes through stages (seven, to be precise) of *consciousness* to the ultimate manifestation of *reason*, each stage representing growth from the preceding stage, but with its own flaws; thus each stage yields to the next. In large part, these stages follow an evolution of a *master/slave* relationship which *Geist* carries within itself. For example, in the fourth stage, the stage of *stoicism*, the slave class compensates for their subjugation by cultivating a sense of a sovereign inner self, a spiritual fortitude that remains unaffected by the outer circumstances of their lives. An obvious limitation of such a creed is that it is vague, abstract, and removed from the life that must be lived. You are still a slave. What follows is a stage Hegel calls *skepticism* – a denial of the reality of the physical world, which of course has its own inadequacies. An elucidation of the *seven stages of consciousness* is beyond the scope of this outline, but the list is as follows: (1) awareness of objects, (2) "struggle unto death," (3) master/slave relationship, (4) stoicism, (5) skepticism, (6) "unhappy consciousness," and (7) reason.

Hegel believed that the final stage had been manifested in the Prussian State, whose culture was *Geist* in all its wonder, both knower and known. True freedom for the individual consisted in the willful submission to the wellbeing of the State. For Hegel, morality was nationalism, plain and simple.

## Commentary: Geist in the Romantic Era (Who You Gonna Call?)

Notice that following Kant's dour warning about the futility of doing metaphysics, the first heavyweight to emerge within the discipline, Georg Hegel, was a profoundly influential metaphysician. His idea of *Geist* (ghost, God, spirit, mind, consciousness), a growing metaphysical entity that manifests itself in a progression of instantiations over time, caught on especially in the literary arts of the Romantic era, especially in America. The American transcendentalists, for example, embraced the idea that we are all parts of God Himself, who knows and creates the world through us. In "The Over-Soul," a title that brings *Geist* immediately to mind, Emerson writes, ". . . the heart in thee is the heart of all; . . . one blood rolls uninterruptedly an endless circulation through all men, as the water of the globe is all one sea, and, truly seen, its tide is one." In Whitman's "Song of Myself," the pronoun in the title could be read in large part as a reference not to Whitman but to the all-inclusive cosmic self. There the poet embraces the impermanence and relativity of truths as well as their contradictory relationships. "Do I contradict myself? / Very well then I contradict myself, / (I am large, I contain multitudes.)" Shades of *Geist* are in Schopenhauers's Will and in Nietzsche's Will to Power (not to mention his wonderful description of the Dionysian and Apollonian sides of Attic tragedy). The concept stretches back to Thales's one (water) vs. many (temporary forms) and forward to the mid-twentieth-century-pop-cultural fad of being "one with everything." We are like waves in the ocean, individuals but part of something larger.

# Marx

*dialectical materialism*
*proletariat*
*bourgeoisie*
*social being*
*species being*
*class society*
*alienation*
*capitalism*
*use value*
*exchange value*
*substructure*
*superstructure*

Hegel had a clear and profound influence on Karl Marx. Both were philosophers of history, and both saw history as teleological. But whereas Hegel saw history as a dialectic of idealism (an organic development of truth itself), Marx's focus was strictly economic, thus resulting in his theory of *dialectical materialism*. For Marx, the oppositional forces in this dialectic were two *classes* of society, the *proletariat* (or working class) and the *bourgeoisie* (or owner class). This antagonistic relationship is the chief obstacle to human fulfillment, and only by eradicating the division of society into classes can the species and the individual be rid of alienation and exploitation.

On a fundamental level, Marx distinguishes between two aspects of human nature, *species being* and *social being*. Our *species being* is such that we have a natural inclination to improve the world, our environment, our society. Our *social being* consists in our inclination to work together, to cooperate. Obviously these two aspects of our existence coincide to the benefit of the community, everyone working together to make the world a better place. The trouble comes when the collective labors of the community create a surplus of goods that requires a select group of people, the *owner class*, to manage the labor and its products of another group, the *labor class*. Thus early in history society became a *class society*. Even at this stage, the problem for the labor class is *alienation*, probably the most important term in Marx's philosophy. The labor class is alienated from (1) the labor itself. Instead of a natural impulse to work to improve the world, labor is now a directive issued by another. You have a boss. In addition, the labor class is alienated from (2) the owner class. The relationship between the two classes lacks the sense of comradery that came naturally before the division of society. And then there is alienation from (3) oneself. As a directive from the boss, labor is no longer something one can identify with. "Don't confuse your career with your life" is a common bit of contemporary advice. Whereas before, one was to an extent what one did, now one's job is what one is forced to do to have their own separate, private life. There now exists, in Marx's words, "a wedge between the two dimensions of the self, the individual and the communal." And elsewhere: "The worker only feels himself outside his work, and in his work he feels outside himself." Historically alienation was limited until the *industrial revolution*, when full-blown *capitalism* brought it (capitalism) to the point of a critical pathology.

## A Marxist Critical Analysis of Capitalism

Not surprisingly, Marx draws a fundamental distinction between two forms of value. (1) The *use value* equals the specific usefulness of X. The use value of a shovel is that I can dig a hole with it. (2) *Exchange value*. I have two shovels, and you have two pots. The value of the second shovel is that I can exchange it for a pot. Its value to me has become partially *abstracted*. Not only can I exchange it for your pot; I could as well exchange it for Jane's hoe if, for example, Jane has no shovel. In other words, the value of the shovel to me is no longer direct, no longer concrete, and to that extent I am alienated from it.

Capital, then, or money, as a pure medium of exchange represents the next level of abstraction of value. Money has no use value to anyone, only exchange value. In fact, money is the pure abstraction of value. But even as the abstraction of value, isn't money – capital – simply a convenience? How insidious? According to Marx, two things happened with the industrial revolution that compounded the alienating effects of capital enormously. (1) Capitalists believed that virtually anything could be monetized, including human beings, their time, and their labor. (2) Capital has the power to increase itself through investment. The combined effect of these two factors amounts to a curious inversion of value. While on one level the value of money lies in its power to purchase goods and services, now the value of virtually everything concrete (including human beings) lies in the amount of money it can bring. Once the *ism* is added to *capital*, it becomes the *basis* of value, not merely a measure. Furthermore, the thoroughgoing capitalist learns that a restraint on spending (for concrete goods and services) in favor of investment yields an increase in value. And like Ebenezer Scrooge, they deny themselves pleasure, living a life of asceticism, slaves to their own wealth. Marx puts it as follows: "Money dethrones all the gods of man and turns them into a commodity. Money is the universal, independently constituted value of all things. It has therefore deprived the whole world, both the world of man and nature, of its own value. Money is the alienated essence of man's work and his being. This alien being rules him and he worships it."

Under full-blown capitalism, the alienation is four-fold: (1) We are alienated from the product of our labors. The old saw about how the cobbler's children go barefoot here pertains. Money separates us from what we make. (2) We are alienated from the labor itself. We become a tool of the factory, of the machine. Especially with division of labor in the factory, it is possible to exhaust oneself with labor and never even see the end product. Our labor is simply the price we pay for our survival. (3) We are alienated from our essence as human beings. As a species we are naturally inclined to improve the world because we are a part of that world. But once that world has been subsumed under the purely abstract value of money, then we cease to find meaning in being a part of the world. (4) Finally, we are alienated from one another. We see one another as competitors or as means to an end, the end of making money.

## Dialectical Materialism

Not surprisingly, Marx distinguishes between two levels of societal structure: (1) the *economic substructure* and (2) the *superstructure.* The substructure comprises *conditions of production* (such as natural resources, access, etc.), *forces of production* (technology, manpower, etc.) and *relations of production* (social arrangement, distribution, etc.) The *superstructure* consists of more abstract features such as the law, religion, art, ideologies, and the like. Central to Marx's critique of capitalism and to his philosophy of history is that *the superstructure is determined by the substructure* (especially the relations of production). More specifically, the predominant cultural values of any given society are such as to benefit the upper class, or bourgeoisie. For example, one of Marx's most well-known statements is that religion is the "opiate of the masses." As an example, he points to the otherworldliness of medieval Christianity, the promise of glory in the afterlife, as the only way the lower classes could tolerate the exploitation by the upper classes (royalty, nobility, etc.) in the here-and-now.

## Commentary: Of the Red Menace

In this country, the spot-on brilliance of Marx's critique has been buried under his vilification as the "father of communism," mainly by a propagandized rabble for whom the term "communist" means nothing more specific than *anti-American*. "Marxist" has become little more than an expletive. And a certain right-leaning persuasion of Protestantism is particularly prone to equate communism with satanism, despite the fact that the earliest Christian communities forsook private property for the practice of communal ownership because they thought it was the Christian thing to do. But the point is that even if true communism never has had, hasn't now, and never will have a chance against human nature -- even if communism were as demonic as its most witless and fervent foes believe -- that doesn't mean that Marx's critique of capitalism is any less incisive about where a culture so committed to free enterprise is most vulnerable to pathology. For a country so religiously capitalist as the United States, what could be a more critical part of education than a recognition of the most dangerous pitfalls of that devotion? Forget communism, but Marx's critique of capitalism should be taught in every school as a kind of warning label for commencement into the American socio-economic machine. Every textbook on economics, business, merchandising, and the like should have a chapter on alienation. MBAs should be granted with lists of possible side effects, including loss of empathy, abstraction of value, a failure of the self to identify with itself, impotence, free-floating anxiety, and a host of other ills familiar to any middle-class denizen of the day.

America, your enemy knows you best. You would do well to listen.

# Phenomenology



*Dasein*
*intentionality*

Kant's critique of reason segues into Hegel's dialectical idealism via the notion of truth as a construct, for Kant by the individual mind and for Hegel by an organic universal *Geist*. And Hegel's dialectical idealism segues into Marx's dialectical materialism via the dynamics of the dialectic. But another development is traceable from the methodology of Descartes to Kant's transcendental search, and on to the phenomenological methods of Husserl and Heidegger.

Remember that for Descartes, certainty in knowledge begins with awareness of the self, the *cogito*. The path of that knowledge then leads from an awareness of one's imperfection to knowledge of the world. And for Kant as well, the transcendental search for the basis of truth is in the critical analysis of the structures of the mind that knows. These structures dictate the conditions for a knowable world, the world of experience, a world of *phenomena*.

*Phenomenology* is a methodology based on the assumption that the only world we can know is, in large part, a product of the mind that knows it. Phenomenology involves a transcendental perspective on oneself as both author and protagonist of the narrative of one's own world.

To put it mildly, accessibility was not uppermost in the minds of the two giants of phenomenology (Husserl and Heidegger). Husserl's vocabulary is densely esoteric and strung together in a style that is meditative and soporific. Heidegger, to his credit, did not trust the essay as an effective medium for philosophy, nor did he trust modern language to express our primal relationship with the world. Heidegger's prose is the result of a deep-mining of the language with an attempt to restore its most primitive poetic function.

*Intentionality* is central to Husserl's pheno-menology; that is, consciousness *intends* a world beyond what is immediately given in experience, a world informed by conceptual, aesthetic, sensory, and other modes of consciousness. We look *through* what we see (hear, feel, etc.) to what we make of it.

If there is a word to immediately associate with Heidegger's phenomenology, it is *Dasein*, but virtually nothing in Heidegger's phenomenology lends itself to concise summary. Sometimes translated as *being in the world, Dasein* has to do with how one's world is necessarily a part of one's awareness as a self and with how one's essence is determined by how one chooses to engage in that world. This emphasis on self and on choice places Heidegger in the company of a group of philosophers known as *existentialists*, and it is with consideration of what these writers' commonalities that this outline will conclude.

# Existentialism

The term *existential* has been overused and misused to the point of becoming virtually useless except in the sense of an "existential threat," meaning a threat to something's existence. Back in the mid-20th century, a certain subculture of pseudointellectuals seized on the term as a way of glorifying any general funk, be it creative impotence, lassitude, or boredom with themselves (because they were in fact boring). Susceptibility to misuse is understandable, given the diversity of philosophers who are now grouped under the term. For example, Sartre was an atheist, Nietzsche proclaimed that "God is dead," and Kierkegaard was a passionate Christian, all for reasons that could rightly be considered *existentialist*. But the concept behind the term is plain enough. It has to do with the uniqueness of *oneself* regarding the relationship between *existence* and *essence*. Specifically, for everything in the world except for oneself, essence precedes existence. But for oneself, the inverse is the case. For oneself, *existence precedes essence*.

The *essence* of a thing consists of all the qualities that allow us to recognize it for what it is as opposed to something else. (Think of Plato's *forms*.) For instance, a flat, horizontal surface is part of the essence of a desk. But even if a desk is black, black would not be part of its essence as a desk because I could paint it white and it would still be a desk. Furthermore, the essence of something dictates what it will *do* under certain circumstances. I know that a desk will support a keyboard in a way that will allow me to use it. If I know that something is a lump of coal, I know that it will burn when raised to a certain temperature. It does what it does because of what it is. Obviously a lump of coal has no choice but to do what a lump of coal does. A lump of coal is not *free* to burn or not to burn. It *is* a lump of coal.

Now, remember that for Plato, for something to exist, it must do so according to its form. In other words, *essence precedes existence* in the sense that essence is the precondition for existence. But the single exception to the necessity for essence as a precondition of existence is *oneself.* One exists. *I* exist. However, unlike a desk or a lump of coal, I am free. There is nothing – no essence – to dictate *what* I am to be or do. I can be a potter, a priest, a liar or a thief, a clerk or a clown. Or not. Still, I exist. And even about my existence I am free to choose, for I can always opt out by choosing suicide. Furthermore, whatever I choose to be (whatever essence I choose for myself), I am at any moment free to cease being whatever I have chosen to be, an option unavailable to, say, a sweetpotato. But this freedom to cease being this or that means that there is still nothing to dictate what I am to be or do. What am I? I don't know. What am I to do? I don't know. I know only that I exist, adrift, a mystery to myself, a free-floating absurdity in a world that makes perfect sense, all except for me. Existentialism is about the fact that my existence precedes my essence, plus all that that entails.

# Nietzsche

*the three metamorphoses of man*
*the overman*
*the death of God*
*eternal recurrence*

While Friedrich Nietzsche predated the term *existentialism* by over half a century, he is considered one of the giants of existentialist thought. In keeping with his view of the human predicament, he offered no grand rational scheme of the world in which human beings might place themselves and thus find meaning for their existence. Much of his work takes the forms of poetry, aphorisms, parables, thought experiments, fantastical *what-ifs?*, riddles, and even jokes. His take on the whole idea of objective truth was brutal, locating its origin in a kind of antilife.

The allegory of "The Three Metamorphoses of Man," from *Thus Spoke Zarathustra*, contains probably the simplest sketch of human development (collective or individual) in Nietzsche's view. The first stage is likened to a *camel*, a beast of burden. This stage requires mandates, dictates, rules, "thou shalts." This is the stage of existence in search of essence. "What am I to do?" one asks. "What am I to be?" This is the stage in which humankind looks to God or the gods. Or the child looks to their parents. Or the masses look to a leader.

The second stage is the *lion*, defiant, ferocious. The lion is the dragon slayer. In the wilderness the lion seeks and slays the dragon of "thou shalt," breaking ties of obedience, freeing itself from God or any other master. This is man the iconoclast, man the revolutionary. Or man the teenager. In this stage, *thou shalt* is replaced by *I will*.

The third stage is the *child*, seeing the world in all its possibility, able to create one's own values, to live by them, and to take full responsibility for oneself. It is a *yes* to life.

Clearly the metamorphosis from the first to the second stage requires courage to face one's own existence. The first stage gave to the self *meaning*, meaning which came from obedience to the master. Nietzsche speaks often of the horror of meeting the ungoverned self. ("But the worst enemy you can meet will always be yourself; you lie in wait for yourself in caverns and forests. Lonely one, you are going the way to yourself!" *TSZ*) But once the horror, the nausea, the pity, the vertigo of meeting oneself are overcome, one is prepared to remake oneself, re-born as it were, to freely create. This third stage makes possible what Nietzsche called the *overman (der Übermensch)*, a term distorted by Adolf Hitler to refer to the Aryan race.

Since so much of Nietzsche's writing consists of metaphor, symbolism, and other intentional ambiguities, much of his language has found its way into popular culture along with gross misunderstandings. For instance, in *The Gay Science*, a madman proclaims, "God is dead." A simplified version of Nietzsche's meaning here is that science has begun to fill the role formerly played by God in the culture. Nietzsche was referring to a pandemic of alienation to come, since God was believed to care about us, but science doesn't. (Remember how the beginning of philosophy itself meant the fading relevance of the gods.) By outgrowing a perceived moral dependency on God, humankind must take moral responsibility for himself. This is an existentialist point.

The often repeated "what doesn't kill me makes me stronger" originated in Nietzsche's *Götzen-Däm- merung* (*Twilight of the Gods*), a part of the *will to power's* welcoming of challenge, obstacles to over- come. And *eternal recurrence* was presented not as a theory of history or cosmology but rather as a thought experiment: live each moment as if it were eternal, not simply a point on the path towards some cosmic resolution where struggle would cease.

# Kierkegaard

*existential modes*
*aesthetic mode*
*ethical mode*
*religious mode*
*the self as subject (as opposed to object)*
*the self as absurd*
*existential despair*
*teleological suspension of the ethical*

The Danish philosopher Søren Kierkegaard shared Nietzsche's mistrust of systematic analyses and constructions as philosophical methods. He sometimes adopted pseudonymous personae to represent various points of view on how to live a life. He believed "objective truth" to be irrelevant to the ultimate human need, which is to find meaning for one's existence, and described his own deepest held convictions as "ineffable." But despite Kierkegaard's mistrust of systems, one can gain a foothold into his thought via his account of the three *existential modes*: the *aesthetic*, the *ethical*, and the *religious*.

But first, on the lot of the *self*: (1) The self is not an object among other objects. The self is *subject(ive)*, knowing objects but not knowable *as* an object. The self cannot be made sense of by *reason* the way any other object can. (2) In other words, the self is *absurd*. (3) And this absurdity of the self, when recognized, becomes the object of *despair*. (For a quick example, consider why boredom is bad. It's because you have no distraction from yourself in your absurdity.)

Thus in the context of the self's absurdity and despair, Kierkegaard discusses three options, three *existential modes* (*modes of existence*): (1) *the aesthetic*, (2) *the ethical*, and (3) *the religious.*

The *aesthete* seeks stimulation, often in the form of entertainment, as a distraction from the anxiety of existence. This mode is essentially a flight from boredom. Sports, adventure, casual sex, gambling, hobbies, daydreams, travel and tv are a few of the countless pastimes that can provide a temporary focus away from oneself and one's despair, but of course *temporary* is the key term that points to the ultimate futility of the attempted escape. Probably the purest form of aesthetic indulgence is with recreational drugs, and like drugs, all forms of aesthetic stimulation eventually begin to wane in effectiveness, leaving one to either increase the amount or degree or to look for a new source of pleasure. But eventually one simply runs out of world (or ODs), the boredom is back worse than ever, and one is again stuck with oneself like the sudden resurfacing of a bad memory.

A person in the *ethical mode* attempts to validate their existence according to a moral code or law. The ethicist looks for meaning in the performance of *duty*. The ethicist wishes to be a *good person* by virtue of the *law*, the *commandments*. (This is the *thou shalt* that Nietzsche's camel seeks.) The law at least temporarily affords a protection against one's absurdity. But this protection is only a form of denial, for the law is objective, public, and therefore irrelevant to one's ultimate subjective predicament. Furthermore, as long as one is free to cease being *good*, then morality provides only a shallow sense of stability. And the longer this freedom goes unrecognized, the more monstrous it becomes.

The third existential mode, the *religious*, is ineffable; that is, it is beyond words. Still, we can begin to get a feel by considering the plight of the self, which is *absurd*. This means that reason itself offers no meaningful perspective. No system, scientific, philosophical, or ethical, will accommodate the existence of the self. The self is subjective and cannot be adequately apprehended as an object. And yet the self *is* one's very self, a mystery and a sufferer of despair.

Consider what it is like to suffer an all-consuming love for another person. Now suppose you recognize that acting on this love would be fatal to any prospect of a life that would be considered decent by any standards of reason, practicality, or even morality. Still, your love is such that reason, practicality, and morality pale in significance when compared to your fundamental (existential) passion for your beloved. The *person* of the beloved transcends any thought, law, or concept. In fact, the person of the beloved transcends truth itself. No principle, concept, or account applies. Any idea, law, or system is beside the point. This is a form of desperation, and it is the only thing commensurate with the naked fact of one's own existence.

In Kierkegaard's case, the beloved was God. He wrote at length about the case of Abraham's *"teleological suspension of the ethical"* mode, by which Abraham's passionate devotion to God led him to go against all Jewish law and ethics to obey God's commandment to kill Isaac. But the point is that to act on anything less than such a passion is ultimately loss and betrayal of the self.

# Sartre

Fundamental to Jean Paul Sartre's place among the existentialists is his distinction between two types of being: *pour soi* (for itself) and *en soi* (in itself). Being *pour soi* is human, conscious, and free, unlike *en soi* in all three respects. Sartre's meditations on consciousness take him from the simplest level, consciousness of objects, to a woeful state of *inauthenticity*. Consciousness must necessarily be of an object which is distinct and separate from one's consciousness of it. Furthermore, in being conscious of the object, one is also *aware (conscious) of oneself* as aware of that object. Hence, consciousness always involves a *gap* between oneself and the world of which one is aware.

From there, through a series of intricate steps, Sartre arrives at an awareness of his own *freedom* from the causally determined world. But this freedom from causation is also a freedom from one's own past. In other words, one is cut loose from any essence, whether causally determined or determined by one's past identity. This untethering of the self from any essence Sartre describes as *"condemned to be free."* There is no real escape from one's freedom. However, a sort of self-deception offers itself. One adopts a role, a part to play, a lens through which to see oneself as *being en soi*. One *is* a professor, or a wife, or a priest, or a consumer. Sartre calls such instances of pretense *bad faith*. It is inauthentic identification as an attempt to escape the awful freedom of one's own existence.

## Commentary: On Faux and Real Despair

Back in the mid-20th century, it was considered cool to be an existentialist. In Paris, in the Saint-Germain-des-Prés cafes, stylish intellectuals liked to sit around wearing scarves and smoking Gitanes and commiserating about despair, while in America the angst fests tended to occur on college campuses and in jazz bars. It was easy enough to feel like you were a part of something that way. Secretly, it felt good to intellectualize your lack of meaning – your nothingness – and thus to identify as an intellectual among intellectuals. You became tight with a community of the alienated. And certainly a word like existentialism lent a sense of loftiness to your plight. It was like irony and Sartrean "bad faith" had fed on each other to the point where the whole scene begged to be satirized by the likes of Woody Allen and Steve Martin. Still, who but the shallowest and the least self-aware has not been rocked to the core by the mystery of one's own existence? By the absurdity of being cast into the world, ultimately alone and on your own? By the awful freedom of choice, a freedom that cuts you loose from any reference but your own nothingness?

Who has not harbored the suspicion that they alone are a complete fake, a mere persona, working to fit in while everyone else knows perfectly well who they are and therefore what to do and what to say? ("She came in and said this, so I just said that, and then that other thing happened, so I did such and such," like billiard balls, reacting to actions in perfect conformity to laws of cause and effect.) Who has not feared being found out, discovered to be nobody, a void at the core, a frightened ghost pretending to be a part of the world?

More than once, at the age of nine or ten, your author would take to the store on allowance day for a bag of candy. There was, on the way, a bridge over a creek, where the author would often sit to watch the water below, sometimes losing himself in the sight and soft rush of the stream. On those allowance days, the author would dangle the bag of candy over the creek, and the thought would occur to him that the only thing keeping him from letting go, dropping the bag, was his own resolve. But in fact, the more conscious he was of that resolve, the less stable it became, for no moment had claim on the next, so that each moment involved a choice: to hold or to release. And thus did the author end up, on several occasions, in an unaccountable burst of freedom, tossing the bag of candy into the creek. And who has not had the horrible thought, driving over a high bridge, of the horrible freedom one has for a spontaneous flick of the wrist on the wheel, and for no good reason except that no moment has a claim on the next? What is there to stop you from suddenly beginning to scream? Who has not been in a business meeting, or in church, or at a wine and cheese party, or a funeral or wedding, or simply at home in the living room with the spouse, and had the thought that one might simply begin to scream, as one would in a nightmare?

# Conclusion: Just a Thought

A pivotal moment in the history of philosophy came when Parmenides denied the reality of change or plurality, in large part on the assumption that language, thought, and reality are isomorphic; that is, if it's real it can be understood, and if it can be understood it can be verbalized. Plato's faith in the language was more qualified in favor of the power of dialogue to bring participants to a shared vision of truth, though that truth may not be explicitly expressible. Kant argued that reason itself is inadequate for access to metaphysical truths, and Wittgenstein (not included in this outline) demonstrated fairly soundly that language itself is inherently closed off from all but a limited scope of truth. Kierkegaard insisted on the ineffability of the religious mode of existence.

In a famous thought experiment, known as *Mary's Room*, a scientist (Mary) is somehow confined since birth to a black and white environment (room) wherein she learns everything there is to know about the *physics* of color, plus the neurophysiology of chromatic experience. The question is: If Mary ever were to step out of her room for the first time and actually see, say, the blue sky, has she learned anything new? The experiment is intended as an argument against the position that all reality is physical.

It seems to me that the scope of this argument could be broadened to other phenomena such as, for example, the aesthetic experience of art. I take it as a matter of course that there occurs a communication of sorts as one listens to, say, the "Albinoni Adagio." A mutual awareness occurs of something beyond the sound itself, something that could neither be expressed in words nor reduced by reason. The same goes for the visual arts and for poetry. (Although poetry is verbal, it is certainly not language as formulation of reasoning.) George Steiner calls these objects of awareness "real presences" in his book of the same title, arguing that they transcend reason and are therefore not reducible by reason. (His overall purpose in the book is to refute all schools of criticism that are not essentially theological.)

However one answers the question of whether Mary gains new knowledge from her first experience of color, it must be admitted that what she gains is unobtainable by any means available in the black and white room. That is the given of the thought experiment. By broadening the experiment to the experience of, say, music, I am suggesting by analogy that there is a kind of *gain* that is unobtainable by any non-musical means. And by further extension, I would suggest that the same is the case with any of the arts, which are, after all, means of both discovery and expression.

Both science and philosophy are means of discovery, distinguished mainly by methodologies. Science employs the scientific method, whereas philosophy tends to rely on pure reason expressed by language. Now, who would deny that art affords a means of discovery and of obtaining a *gain* as real as Mary's first experience of the color blue? This gain is necessarily aesthetic, but as a gain it is no less real than knowledge gained by science or philosophy.

My point is that while philosophy and science are subject to certain confinements (comparable to Mary's black and white room), art (and perhaps other pursuits) may provide windows on other realms of the real inaccessible by science or philosophy. As Hamlet puts it, "There are more things in Heaven and Earth, Horatio, than are dreamt of in your philosophy."

A philosopher with no knowledge of science is not likely to fare well in their chosen field. Likewise, a scientist who turns a deaf ear to philosophical questions is at best operating in a vacuum and at worst dangerous. I submit that any philosopher or scientist who has no aesthetic sensibility is working with a significant handicap in the quest for knowledge. I would submit further that any such philosopher or scientist who eschews trying to cultivate such a sensibility is in effect simply protecting their ignorance.

**Donald Mangum** is retired from teaching English and philosophy. He has published a novella, *The Roar Beneath* (Main Street Rag Publishing Co., 2016), and a number of short stories and poems in *The New Yorker, Confrontation, The Mississippi Review, Home Planet News,* and other periodicals.

The cover image is a reproduction of *The Walking Philosopher,* an anonymous hand-colored etching, circa 1800.

www.ingramcontent.com/pod-product-compliance
Lightning Source LLC
Chambersburg PA
CBHW051545050726
47595CB00002B/647